TRAINS

L **HAMMOND World Atlas**
Part of the Langenscheidt Publishing Group

Published in the United States and its territories and Canada by
HAMMOND WORLD ATLAS CORPORATION
Part of the Langenscheidt Publishing Group
36-36 33rd Street, Long Island City, NY 11106

EXECUTIVE EDITOR: Nel Yomtov

EDITOR: Kevin Somers

Produced for Hammond World Atlas Corporation by

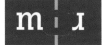

MOSELEY ROAD INC.
129 MAIN STREET
IRVINGTON, NY 10533
WWW.MOSELEYROAD.COM

MOSELEY ROAD INC.
PUBLISHER Sean Moore
ART DIRECTORS Brian MacMullen
EDITORIAL DIRECTOR Lisa Purcell

EDITORS Lisa Purcell, Amber Rose
PHOTO RESEARCHER Ben DeWalt
DESIGNER Joanne Flynn
CARTOGRAPHY Neil Dvorak
EDITORIAL ASSISTANT Rachael Lanicci

COVER DESIGN Linda Kosarin

Printed and bound in Canada

ISBN-13: 978-0841-614963

TRAINS

119

JANE SHIMAMOTO

HAMMOND World Atlas
Part of the Langenscheidt Publishing Group

Contents

Trains on Track

What goes from 30 miles (48 km) per hour to more than 250 (402 km) in just over a century and a half? It's the train.

Starting in the early nineteenth century in Great Britain and the United States, railroads blossomed quickly, spreading across the continental United States and around the world as steam power took off. The Golden Age of Rail (around the turn of the twentieth century) spurred economic development, changed the face of the countryside, and affected everything from casual travel to wars waged across entire continents.

Steam power ruled the rails for more than 100 years, but in the mid-twentieth century, different kinds of power and brand-new kinds of trains started rolling along the railroad tracks.

Today's trains, especially in Europe and Asia, are transportation superheroes, pulling enormous loads of heavy materials, rushing travelers more than 200 miles (322 km) per hour, and riding on only a single rail. Some trains even float, powered by a kind of magnet.

In the history of train travel, there are no shortage of characters, heroes, and villains—not to mention a few spectacular robberies, rescues, and wrecks. So grab your ticket and climb aboard for a trip on the wonderful world of trains!

Signals such as this one stand at sites where roads cross train tracks, letting drivers know when it's safe to cross.

An old-fashioned steam locomotive. Powered by steam produced by boiling water in the engine, locomotives were once common sights on the world's railroads.

Freight trains carry heavy loads of goods, such as coal, iron, and steel. Freight trains don't move very fast, but they are some of the world's longest and most powerful trains.

The best places to hop on passenger trains are at well-kept stations, such as this one in Barcelona, Spain.

Trains Around the World

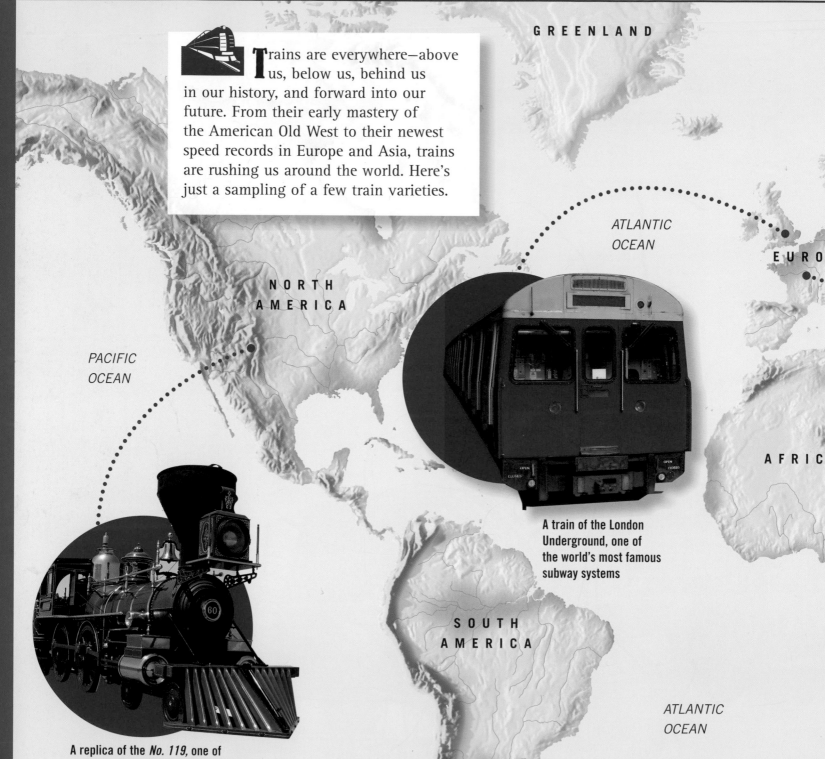

Trains are everywhere—above us, below us, behind us in our history, and forward into our future. From their early mastery of the American Old West to their newest speed records in Europe and Asia, trains are rushing us around the world. Here's just a sampling of a few train varieties.

GREENLAND

ATLANTIC OCEAN

EUROPE

NORTH AMERICA

PACIFIC OCEAN

AFRICA

A train of the London Underground, one of the world's most famous subway systems

SOUTH AMERICA

ATLANTIC OCEAN

A replica of the *No. 119,* one of two famous locomotives that met each other on May 10, 1869, at Promontory Summit, Utah, completing the First Transcontinental Railroad

The TGV, or *Train à Grande Vitesse* (French for "high-speed train"), carries passengers all over France at speeds approaching 200 miles (322 km) per hour. It is the world's fastest train on wheels.

А в 132

Russia's Trans-Siberian Railway has been bringing people and goods to some of Asia's most remote areas since the 1890s.

A S I A

JAPAN

PACIFIC OCEAN

Australia runs some of the world's most powerful freight locomotives, like this SCT class powerhouse.

SCT 004

SCT004

Japanese commuters get around on the Shinkansen, a network of high-speed railway lines operated by four Japan Railways Group companies. The Tokaido Shinkansen is the busiest high-speed rail line in the world.

A U S T R A L I A

INDIAN OCEAN

PACIFIC OCEAN

Horse-Drawn Transport

 Which came first, the railroad or the train? The answer may surprise you: it's the railroad! Long before anyone had thought of a caboose or a steam engine, people laid rails to help transport goods from place to place. Starting in the sixteenth century in Europe, such transport systems, called wagonways or tramways, allowed horses to pull wagons with greater ease and efficiency than they could on bumpy, unpaved roads. By the eighteenth century, inventors started to wonder if they could devise an engine that was even stronger than a horse—and the first steam engines were born.

Below, horses pull carriages along tracks in front of the Paleis op de Dam in Amsterdam, the Netherlands, in the nineteenth century.

Gone but Not Forgotten

During the era of the steam engine, the locomotive widely took over the business of carrying people and freight from draft horses, earning the nickname "Iron Horse." But the Iron Horse owed more than just its name to its equine counterpart. In the 1780s, Scottish engineer and inventor James Watt, who worked on improving steam engines, coined the term "horsepower" to describe how powerful steam engines were compared to powerful draft horses. Even today, manufacturers describe train engines, car engines, and many other kinds of motors in terms of horsepower (hp).

ROUND AND ROUND WE GO

THE HOMES FOR EARLY LOCOMOTIVES, called roundhouses, are large covered structures hugging a turntable in a semicircle. The first locomotives couldn't easily move in reverse, so a roundhouse's turntable would rotate a locomotive for its return trip. Switching—the process of putting trains behind a locomotive—would also take place in a roundhouse. In Maryland, the Baltimore & Ohio Railroad houses its museum in a 22-sided roundhouse built in 1884.

At right, locomotives stand ready in the curved roundhouse at the top left of the photo. To turn the locomotives around or maneuver them onto different tracks, an engineer drove onto the turntable, shown at center, which then rotated to a new position.

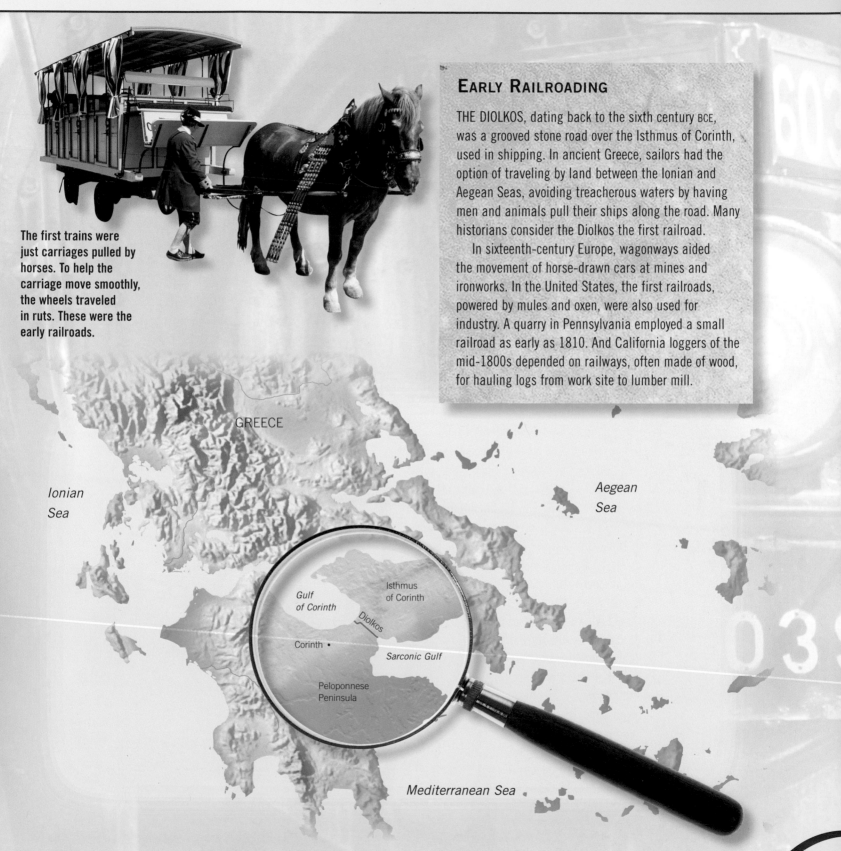

The first trains were just carriages pulled by horses. To help the carriage move smoothly, the wheels traveled in ruts. These were the early railroads.

EARLY RAILROADING

THE DIOLKOS, dating back to the sixth century BCE, was a grooved stone road over the Isthmus of Corinth, used in shipping. In ancient Greece, sailors had the option of traveling by land between the Ionian and Aegean Seas, avoiding treacherous waters by having men and animals pull their ships along the road. Many historians consider the Diolkos the first railroad.

In sixteenth-century Europe, wagonways aided the movement of horse-drawn cars at mines and ironworks. In the United States, the first railroads, powered by mules and oxen, were also used for industry. A quarry in Pennsylvania employed a small railroad as early as 1810. And California loggers of the mid-1800s depended on railways, often made of wood, for hauling logs from work site to lumber mill.

GREECE

Ionian Sea

Aegean Sea

Gulf of Corinth

Isthmus of Corinth

Diolkos

Corinth •

Sarconic Gulf

Peloponnese Peninsula

Mediterranean Sea

Full Steam Ahead

While Americans were still celebrating the expansion of horse-drawn railways, British inventor George Stephenson had moved on, full steam ahead. In 1825, his steam-powered engine, the *Locomotion*, hauled 30 cars of freight on England's Stockton & Darlington Railway. Stephenson would eventually triumph with the *Rocket*, in a kind of steam-off competition to earn the right to design engines for the Liverpool & Manchester Railway. The *Rocket* lived up to its name, reaching speeds of approximately 28 miles (45 km) per hour (a horse can run faster, but not for long—and not while pulling heavy loads).

A Railroad's Best Friend

Back in the United States, the South Carolina Canal and Rail Road Company got the message. They launched the *Best Friend of Charleston* on December 25, 1830. It was the first steam-powered railroad open to passengers. The 6-mile ride dazzled the 141 adventurers that Christmas day. One car also carried mail, another historic first. Though an explosion felled the historic *Best Friend* a year later, the South Carolina Canal and Rail Road Company had more trains on more tracks by 1833. Steam power sent wagon horses back to the barn.

RICHARD TREVITHICK

LONG BEFORE the Wright brothers achieved flight at Kitty Hawk, transportation inventors struggled long and hard to create an engine that would replace horse-drawn rail travel. British inventor Richard Trevithick, already known for his advances in engine design, made history in 1804. One of his engines successfully pulled 10 tons (9.1 metric tons) of iron along the Merthyr Tydfil Tramroad from Penydarren to Abercynon, Wales, a distance of 9.75 miles (15.7 km)—a genuine locomotive! Unfortunately, the rails, meant for lighter loads, cracked under the weight of Trevithick's invention. Multiple runs would not be possible. Nearly 10 more years passed before a locomotive was successfully paired with more durable tracks.

A high-pressure steam engine, built by Richard Trevithick in 1806. Although Trevithick did not invent the use of steam power, his engines were steam power's earliest successes.

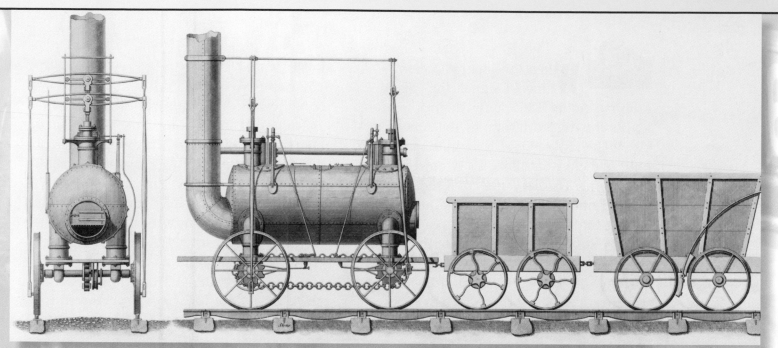

A diagram of George Stephenson's invention, the steam locomotive, shown pulling railroad cars

The *Tom Thumb* may have been small, but it had a large impact on the future of train travel. Only three years old when the *Tom Thumb* ran its race, the Baltimore & Ohio Railroad moved fully to steam power.

PETER COOPER'S "TOM THUMB" 1829-30 BALTIMORE & OHIO R. R.

THE *TOM THUMB*

IN 1829, wealthy factory owner Peter Cooper constructed a locomotive that was quite a sight—boiler tubes made out of old gun barrels and a remarkably small chassis (the metal frame). In fact, the locomotive was so small, that Cooper named it the *Tom Thumb*, after the tiny man of English folklore. The next year, Cooper accepted a challenge to race the *Tom Thumb* against a horse-drawn car along a 13-mile (21 km) stretch of the Baltimore & Ohio Railroad.

Spectators lined the route to witness this historic matchup. Cooper produced a scorching-hot fire, and soon the steam propelled the *Tom Thumb* ahead of the horse. A malfunction brought the *Tom Thumb* to a stop before the finish line, but Cooper had proved that the future did not run on four legs. Thirty years after that memorable race, Cooper established a college in New York City to educate artists, architects, and engineers at no cost. Founded in 1859, the Cooper Union is still tuition-free today!

The First Transcontinental Railroad

When President Abraham Lincoln signed the Pacific Railroad Act of 1862, only wagons ventured across the rugged terrain of the American West. The journey was long and hard, and only one city—Salt Lake City—graced the mountains. The act authorized the United States to build the first railroad across the entire continent. Two new railroad companies quickly stepped up: Central Pacific would travel eastward from Sacramento, California, and the Union Pacific would meet it on its way westward from Omaha, Nebraska.

The Sierra Nevada Mountains nearly bested the railroads. Theodore Judah was certain a way could be found, and he located it in Donner Pass, below.

Trouble in the Wild West

The outbreak of the Civil War in 1861 complicated the project. The war caused shortages of iron, wood, and able-bodied men—all necessary to lay tracks. The work was grueling and slow. Blizzards in 1866 turned the masons and mechanics into snow removers. The passage through the Sierra Nevada Mountains alone required the creation of 15 tunnels. American Indians, who saw the railroad as a threat to their way of life, challenged the Union Pacific's drive westward. Most people believed it was impossible to dig through the mountains, and, indeed, it nearly was.

THEODORE JUDAH

IT TOOK YOUNG THEODORE JUDAH more than a decade to get anyone to share his vision of a transcontinental railroad. In 1860, Judah finally found four supporters in Sacramento, California: Leland Stanford, Collis P. Huntington, Mark Hopkins, and Charles Crocker. Known as the Big Four, they, with Judah, set up the Central Pacific Railroad in less than a year. An engineer by training, Judah concluded a railroad could navigate the Sierra Nevada Mountains through the Donner Pass. Although names like Abraham Lincoln and Leland Stanford are most closely associated with this national wonder, it was Theodore Judah who made the whole thing work.

Theodore Judah died in 1863, six years before his dream of a transcontinental railroad came true.

Fire in the Mountains

A literal breakthrough came in 1867, when the Central Pacific Railroad began using nitroglycerine, an explosive, to blast through the mountains. The dangerous substance made the difficult work go much faster—but it caused many extra deaths. Finally, in 1869, the work ended at Promontory Summit in Utah: the country's East and West were truly united for the first time.

THE GOLDEN SPIKE

THE GOLDEN SPIKE, weighing a little less than a pound, was adorned with an engraving commemorating the American Civil War, which ended less than five years earlier. One side of the spike reads, MAY GOD CONTINUE THE UNITY OF OUR COUNTRY AS THE RAILROAD UNITES THE TWO GREAT OCEANS OF THE WORLD. The words THE LAST SPIKE appear on its top. Leland Stanford hammered the commemorative spike on May 10, 1869. The Union Pacific was running and on schedule in only five days' time.

Leland Stanford, center, drives the last spike into the ground. Hundreds of spectators attended the ceremony of the Golden Spike.

Below, the progress of the First Transcontinental Railroad

First Transcontinental Railroad
→ Central Pacific
← Union Pacific
● cities

Oregon · Idaho · Wyoming · California · Nevada · Utah · Nebraska · Kansas · Colorado

Driving of the Golden Spike May 10, 1869

April 13, 1868 Donner Pass

Construction begins October 26, 1863 — Sacramento

Lake Tahoe · Sierra Nevada Mountains

Great Salt Lake · Salt Lake City · Promontory Summit

July 21, 1868 Fort Steele · Rawlins · Rocky Mountains · Continental Divide

Construction begins July 10, 1865

Platte River · Omaha · Wasatch Range

ALL ABOARD!

In the late 1800s, a combination of amazing inventions and little government oversight of business made a few lucky men wealthy beyond all measure. Known for its extreme displays of this new wealth, the era became known as the Gilded Age (*gilded* means "covered with gold"). The railways, sprouting everywhere across the country, created some of these great fortunes, as Americans boarded trains for a new life in distant corners, or simply for pleasure.

Gilded Railroads

It was an age of rapid growth, invention, and luxury. Sharp businessmen like Jay Gould, Cornelius Vanderbilt, and Leland Sanford became some of the nation's first multimillionaires. Tireless inventor George Westinghouse patented 361 inventions, the most critical of which related to railroad mechanics and safety. And George Pullman's belief that travel should reflect the elegance of the time made his the first name in train cars. Between business tycoons and clever engineers, the railroad men of the late 1800s drove the United States into a sparkling new era.

COMMODORE VANDERBILT

HOW DOES $167.4 billion sound? According to *Forbes* magazine's estimate, that is Cornelius Vanderbilt's worth in 2008 dollars. Vanderbilt, born in 1794, earned his vast wealth over a lifetime of investments in steamboats and trains. Vanderbilt's success in the steamboat business inspired the nickname "Commodore" (the highest naval rank at that time).

By the end of his life in 1877, the Commodore had become king of the rails in bustling New York, through smart acquisitions of rival train lines. By 1918, the Vanderbilt train empire stretched as far east as Massachusetts and as far west as Illinois.

DID YOU KNOW?

Cornelius Vanderbilt didn't like trains at first. That's because he was injured in one of the earliest U.S. train accidents, which occurred on November 9, 1833, near Hightstown, New Jersey.

A map of the vast train system owned by Cornelius Vanderbilt in 1893. The thick black lines are the railroad routes covered by Vanderbilt's New York Central and Hudson River Railroads.

A reconstruction of the Union Pacific's *No. 119* locomotive, present at the historic completion of the First Transcontinental Railroad, puffs away during a demonstration in Utah's Golden Spike National Historic Site.

LELAND STANFORD AND THE GOLDEN SPIKE

BORN IN WATERVLIET, NEW YORK, in 1824, Leland Stanford sought fortune in the West, selling goods in California's mining camps. With an eye on his eastern roots and a nation recovering from civil war, Stanford saw an opportunity to bring the country together, one track at a time. The Central Pacific Railroad stretched from Sacramento, California, to the Union Pacific's western end at Promontory Summit, in what became the state of Utah. That's a total of 1,776 miles (2,858 km) of track. Completed in 1869, the railroads made fast, comfortable coast-to-coast travel a reality. Stanford, the Union Pacific's president, marked the occasion with the now-legendary Golden Spike. Sixteen years later, he provided the endowment for what became Stanford University, one of the highest-ranking colleges in the country.

Leland Stanford served as governor of California from 1862 to 1863.

All the Livelong Day

The best job for a rail worker during the Golden Age of Rail (late nineteenth to early twentieth centuries) was the engineer's job. When not behind the controls, the engineer supervised the rest of the train's team of onboard employees. The person in charge of the train was called the conductor. He did much of his job in the last car, which was known as the caboose. Here, the rear train crew rested, slept, and did their work.

Hazards Ahead

Whether engineer or brakeman, the men on the train had little say over the management of the railroad. Much of their work was dangerous. To stop a train, brakemen had to race from car to car, turning handbrakes one at a time. They would often have to help a slowing train by climbing in between or on top of train cars. Many brakemen lost their fingers, or slammed into an overpass, resulting in severe injury or death.

Link-and-pin couplers, which connected train cars together, often maimed or crushed brakemen who placed themselves between two meeting cars to slip the pin into the link. In addition, steam trains were hot, and the tracks were often dangerous—especially if the trains had to cross bridges or mountains. Working on the rails was no easy ride!

A railroad worker does his job on a steam-powered locomotive. Hot and prone to explosions, steam locomotives could kill or injure the men who drove or worked on them.

DID YOU KNOW?

In 1925, the African American men who made up the Pullman Porter workforce began organizing into a union, headed by labor organizer A. Philip Randolph. The Brotherhood of Sleeping Car Porters fought for living wages, and when Pullman Company representatives sat down at the bargaining table 10 years later, it was a milestone in the struggle for civil rights.

A. Philip Randolph

SAFETY FIRST

IN 1874, a former Civil War chaplain named Lorenzo Coffin saw a brakeman lose two fingers. It drove Coffin to make this rugged profession safer. He took nightmarish tales of working the rails to the politicians in Washington, D.C. The U.S. Congress passed the Railroad Safety Appliance Act in 1893. It forced railway managers to adopt costly but basic improvements such as George Westinghouse's air brake and inventor Eli Janney's knuckle coupler, which eliminated pins and kept brakemen out of harm's way.

A brakeman on the Chicago & North Western Railway Company in the 1940s. Stopping a steam-powered train took strength, resourcefulness, and a lot of bravery.

DID YOU KNOW?

During the creation of the First Transcontinental Railroad, the construction managers of the Union Pacific and Central Pacific felt a keen sense of competition, sometimes setting superhuman goals for their laborers. In April 1869, workers for the Central Pacific laid down 10 miles (16 km) of track in one day!

Building railroads was even more dangerous than working on trains in the nineteenth century. Contending with heat, rock slides, explosive materials, and brutal management—among other things—thousands of railroad builders died while on the job.

Railroad Strikes

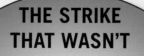

The backbreaking work of building the United States' earliest railroads fell in large part to Chinese and Irish immigrants, who often couldn't find other work due to discrimination. When railroads were up and running, African American men became a significant part of the workforce.

Management could be ruthless. In 1867, Chinese laborers called a strike, demanding higher pay ($40 a month). Charles Crocker, the construction manager of the Central Pacific Railroad, cut off the workers' food supply, and seven days later, the starving strikers went back to work. Trains were crucial to commerce, so the stakes were always high when labor and management came to the negotiating table. Workers found strength in numbers, and, in the late nineteenth century, formed unions. By operating as a large unit, the unionized workforce could deal with management on more equal ground—and if management became too unreasonable, the unions would simply stop working. This kind of work stoppage is called a strike.

Below, the Illinois National Guard watches over the Arcade Building in Pullman, as strikers picket during the Pullman Railroad Strike.

THE STRIKE THAT WASN'T

During President Franklin D. Roosevelt's third term in office, railroad unions demanding wage increases called for a strike to begin on December 7, 1941. Roosevelt's intervention helped unions win their pay hike on December 2. No one knew then that in five days' time, the country would suffer one of its greatest tragedies: the Japanese attack on Pearl Harbor, which thrust the United States into World War II.

U.S. president Franklin D. Roosevelt, leaving Washington, D.C., on the Atlantic Coast Line Presidential Special Railroad

THE PULLMAN STRIKE

DURING A SERIOUS ECONOMIC DOWNTURN in 1894, the Pullman Palace Car Company drastically cut wages for workers. Pullman employees went on strike without consulting their union bosses (this is called a wildcat strike). Shortly after May 11, when the strike began, all train traffic west of Chicago came to a standstill. Ultimately, 50,000 rail workers would participate, and the Pullman Company lost $250,000 every day of the strike. Strike-related violence killed 13 people and injured many more. The union did win partially: the U.S. government forced Pullman to give up the company-owned town of Pullman, Illinois.

THE GREAT RAILROAD STRIKE OF 1877

TO REDUCE COSTS in economically troubled times, the Baltimore & Ohio Railroad (B&O) cut workers' wages twice in a 12-month span. In response, B&O employees in West Virginia went on strike. The strike action mushroomed, marked by rallies and riots. The strike greatly affected Baltimore, Pittsburgh, Chicago, and St. Louis, as strikers found supporters from other railroads, at factories, and even among members of state and federal troops, sent by President Rutherford B. Hayes to confront the unrest. Though more than 100,000 workers took part in the month-long strike, federal troops put an end to it (despite any sympathizers in the ranks), with labor failing to win a single concession.

Scenes from the Great Railroad Strike of 1877. Above, the destruction of Union Depot, Pittsburgh, Pennsylvania, July 21–22; below, the Maryland National Guard Sixth Regiment battles strikers in the streets of Baltimore, Maryland, July 20.

The Great Railroad Strike of 1877

- affected states
- city

The Heavyweights

In the years before railroads became commonplace, settlers on the frontier depended on wagon freighters for tools and provisions. Oxen, pulling a fully laden wagon, can only travel about 10 miles (16 km) per day, so even short trips (from the gold mines of the Sierra Nevada Mountains to San Francisco, for example) could take weeks.

Freight Trains

Trains carrying materials—called freight trains—made an instant impact on the shipment of goods, but for a time, train companies worked hand-in-hand with the old wagons. Trains made hauling faster, but railroads were vulnerable to fire, theft, and accident. Freight rates were regulated by the Interstate Commerce Commission, created by Congress in 1887. Railroads such as the Atchison, Topeka & Santa Fe carried passengers across the plains, but their main source of income was freighting.

In the early twentieth century, the introduction of refrigerated cars boosted the industry. Refrigeration allowed perishable goods—like citrus fruits and dairy products—to travel far and wide. Today, freight trains travel the world over.

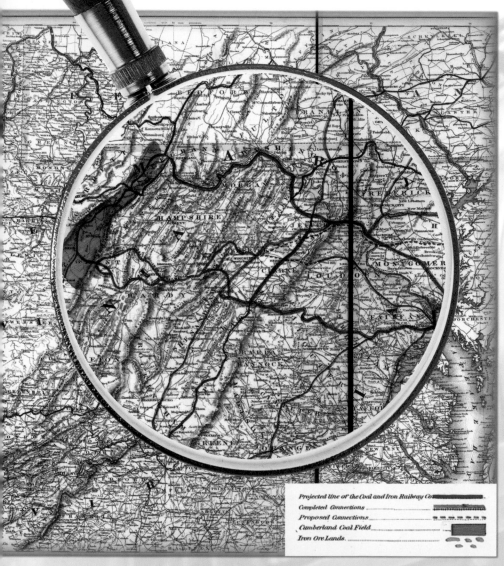

An 1882 map of the Coal & Iron Railroad Company. Locations of coal fields and iron deposits are marked, because they helped dictate the best route for the company's freight trains.

THE BIGGER THE BETTER

BHP BILLITON, the largest mining company in the world, is responsible for the heaviest and longest train ever. Both records were broken on a single day, June 21, 2001, when a train weighing 220 tons (200 metric tons) left from the remote Yandi mines on a 171-mile (275 km) trip through Western Australia. From end to end, the freight train (carrying iron ore) measured approximately 4.5 miles (7.2 km) long.

Another train of astounding length and weight operates through the Sahara Desert in the African nation of Mauritania. The train, also carrying iron ore, is 1.5 miles (2.4 km) long, pulling up to 220 cars and 22,000 tons (19,960 metric tons). Only two or three cars are meant for passengers, often not enough to satisfy demand. Mauritanians eager to head toward the port city of Nouadhibou risk exposure to the elements and jump in "hoppers" for a free, but precarious, 17-hour ride.

A hobo hitches a ride under a boxcar.

ON THE TRACKS

THE GROWING RAIL SYSTEM in the 1800s provided migrant workers both job opportunities and the means to travel to work sites. A community of skilled and unskilled workers developed inside this system. Called hoboes, they stowed away on a train's freight cars and would walk—or jump!—off where they thought they could find work. The hobo's life was one of hardship and rough survival, but it also promised freedom and endless new horizons.

A freight train lugs its load of iron through the rugged Australian outback.

A New Fuel

 A French-born inventor and engineer, Rudolf Diesel put his study of thermodynamics (turning heat into power) to use in developing his most famous invention. In the late nineteenth century, aiming to create a more efficient engine, Diesel designed his first models to run on peanut oil. Unlike gasoline engines, which include spark plugs to ignite fuel, the diesel engine creates extreme heat inside a chamber and mixes the heat with fuel. Diesel engines are remarkably

A diesel engine. Since its invention, diesel has been used to power many types of automobiles—especially trucks—and airplanes as well as train locomotives.

A commemorative stamp pictures Rudolf Diesel and his revolutionary diesel engine.

fuel-efficient and highly useful for freight vehicles. By the 1940s, steam engines were out and diesel engines were in.

Inside a Diesel Engine

When railroads moved from steam to diesel-fuel locomotives, it meant leaving external-combustion engines behind. Early locomotives required somebody to fill a large boiler with coal or wood nearly continuously. The locomotives also had to make numerous stops to procure a constant supply of water and fuel to maintain

DID YOU KNOW?

Rudolf Diesel, famous in his time, traveled extensively to lecture. He was on his way to attend a meeting in England in 1913 when he disappeared from an English Channel steamer. The how and why of his demise, at age 55, is still debated today.

A diesel train

the heat. This method is called external combustion, because the fires are located outside of the engine. A diesel engine compresses air and fuel inside a chamber to create enough heat to get the engine going. Because this happens inside the engine, it is known as internal combustion. By the 1950s, many railroads added an electric component to their diesel trains, making train travel much more efficient.

DID YOU KNOW?

The fourth of 14 children, Werner von Siemens was a legend in the field of electrical engineering. Though his early triumphs were in telegraph communication, the company that still bears his name demonstrated the first electric railway at the Berlin Trade Fair in 1879.

Werner von Siemens

An example of a 4-6-4 locomotive from Australia

WHYTE NOTATION

ENGINEER FREDERICK METHVEN WHYTE (1865–1941) created the numbered classification system for locomotives predominantly used in the United States. "Whyte notation" refers to the wheel arrangement underneath the locomotive. The Hudson locomotive of the *Empire State Express* in New York, for example, was a 4-6-4 locomotive. That is, the locomotive had four leading wheels, six driving wheels, and four trailing wheels. Leading wheels support the front end and handle curves; driving wheels are directly powered by steam and often have the familiar coupling rods attached. Trailing wheels are essential for rear support, often for the cab holding the crew. Longer hauls and heavier loads mean more wheels. The massive Challenger locomotives of the Union Pacific were 4-6-6-4 locomotives, otherwise known as "Big Boys."

707

CITY OF MELBOURNE

R707

leading wheels   driving wheels   trailing wheels

Riding the Rails

Trials and tragedy marked early train travel. Crashes and derailments plagued the system. Fires broke out regularly. In response, train designers tinkered with the shape and size of smokestacks to reduce spark-induced blazes. A pair of major threats to safety was addressed by two *S*'s—swivel and switchback. On a swivel train, four wheels were mounted on a swiveling platform below the engine, helping the train hug the rails around a curve. Switchback tracks force a train to stop if the train starts rolling backward as an engine tries to pull it toward a summit.

Rough Trip

By the late 1800s, train designers had made many improvements, but a rail journey could still be rough. Arriving European immigrants squeezed into the cars of the New York Central, heading to cities such as Pittsburgh and Buffalo. With no running water and hard wooden benches, the cars left passengers cold and sore. Boilers provided some heat but posed a fire risk.

DID YOU KNOW?

The phrase "wrong side of the tracks" comes from early rail travel. Wood-burning engines produced so much smoke, settlers avoided downwind areas. The land with the sootiest air was left to the very poor.

Atchison, Topeka & Santa Fe Railway

— route of the Atchison, Topeka & Santa Fe Railway

● major stop

• cities

The Wealthy Rails

Plush Pullman cars offered comfort for those who could afford it. For the super rich, George Pullman went all out. He appointed private cars with marble bathtubs and solid-gold bathroom fixtures. Railroad baron Jay Gould held multiple private cars to suit his traveling employees. Up until the middle of the twentieth century, money made all the difference when you rode the rails!

Above, a late-nineteenth-century Pullman car, featuring plush seats, carpeting, and overhead lighting. At left, passengers board a train at a station in Ottawa, Canada, in 1909.

THE *SUPER CHIEF*

AFTER THE HARDSHIPS of World War I (1914–1918), Americans again sought luxury train travel. The Atchison, Topeka & Santa Fe Railway aimed to capitalize on the attractions of Southern California. The peak of comfort and prestige for its time, the *Super Chief* serviced tourists and the Hollywood film community. With the automotive industry eating into profits, the Santa Fe introduced the faster, modernized *Super Chief* in 1937. The nine-car train included a post office, dining car, a barbershop, and a cocktail lounge with a Navajo rug. The name of the train, and those of its cars (*Taos* and *Cochiti*, for example) paid tribute to the American Indian lands along its Chicago-to-California route.

The *Super Chief* as it appeared in 1943

Trains and Stations

A SEPTA (Southeastern Pennsylvania Transportation Authority) train. SEPTA serves 3.8 million commuters in the Philadelphia, Pennsylvania, area.

By the mid-twentieth century, many people fled crowded cities to make their homes in the newly named "suburbia" just outside them. In many places, these suburban residents traveled around by car. In high-density areas, such as New York City, however, there wasn't any room to build enough roads. For New York suburbanites, the solution was the train system. Today, millions of people around the world take trains from their hometowns to their jobs in the city—or sometimes vice versa, from homes in the city to the suburbs. These people—called commuters—may also travel from one city to another. This is especially true in Europe, where distances are small, and in places like the mid-Atlantic states in the United States, where commuters might travel from one city—such as Wilmington, Delaware, to another—such as Washington, D.C., or Philadelphia, Pennsylvania.

Many metropolitan areas don't have significant commuter railroads, depending instead on car traffic, but for those that do, trains remain a major part of life. For many of these cities, the stations that commuters travel into have become major landmarks and meeting places—even for people who don't regularly ride the rails.

UNION STATION, WASHINGTON, D.C.

WHEN IT OPENED IN 1908, Union Station was the largest train station in the world. The white granite structure fits seamlessly with the city's other gleaming attractions, such as the Washington Monument (completed in 1884) and the Lincoln Memorial, which opened in 1922. Neglected for years, as air travel became dominant, a renovation of Union Station was completed in 1981. Just before his inauguration (when the president takes his oath of office) in January 2009, President Barack Obama headed to Union Station from Philadelphia, boarding the 70-year-old private Pullman car called the *Georgia 300*, which former presidents George Bush and Bill Clinton had also used.

Union Station attracts more than 32 million visitors every year and has appeared in many movies and television shows, including *Mr. Smith Goes to Washington* and *The West Wing*.

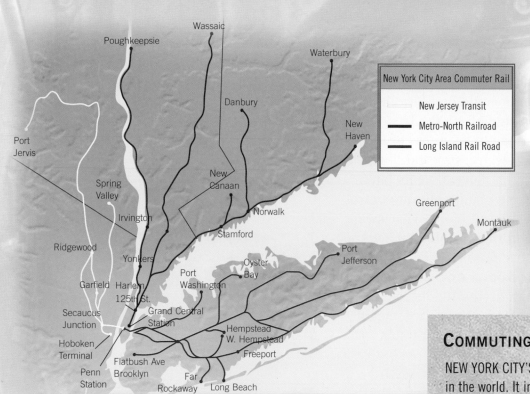

New York City Area Commuter Rail

- New Jersey Transit
- Metro-North Railroad
- Long Island Rail Road

A Metro-North train pulls into a station along its busy New York commuter route.

COMMUTING IN NEW YORK

NEW YORK CITY'S commuter system is one of the largest in the world. It includes several railways, including the Long Island Rail Road, Metro-North Railroad, and New Jersey Transit. The Long Island Rail Road began operating in 1834 as a horse-drawn operation. It is now the busiest commuter railroad in North America, running 735 trains a day. The Metro-North Railroad, connecting New York City with suburban communities and several college towns, runs through several New York State counties and parts of Connecticut. Some of its routes can be traced back to the mid-nineteenth century.

CENTRAL STATION, HELSINKI, FINLAND

A LOCAL ARCHITECT by the name of Eliel Saarinen built his reputation on the design of this wonder, opened in Helsinki, Finland, in 1919. The pink granite structure certainly catches the eye, with four muscular statues standing imposingly under a clock tower. Eliel's son Eero was also a noted architect, who designed the famed St. Louis Gateway arch in Missouri.

Central Station is one of Helsinki's most recognized landmarks, and it has been renovated and upgraded several times, most recently in 2003.

Under the Earth

Thomas Edison is synonymous with electric invention, but without Frank J. Sprague—an Edison contemporary—there would be no trolley cars or subways. At the age of 30, the U.S. Naval Academy graduate saw the success of his design for the first electric streetcar, located in Richmond, Virginia. Several years later, Sprague developed multiple unit control for early subway trains. That meant the motorman could manage the electric power for each train car from a single control. In simplifying the mechanics, Sprague's invention meant the end of steam trains for urban transport.

Since Sprague's death in 1934, subways and other forms of rapid transit—including streetcars, electric light rail, and elevated trains—have become a way of life in more than 150 cities around the world. In New York City alone, 8.5 million passengers ride the railroad, subways, and public bus system every day of the workweek.

DID YOU KNOW?

An innovator in elevator technology, as well train mechanics, Frank Sprague's lack of fame compared to Thomas Edison surely influenced the title of a book by Sprague's wife, Harriet: *Frank J. Sprague and the Edison Myth*.

A postcard from the 1920s features electric streetcars in Richmond, Virginia. In 1887–88, Frank J. Sprague had installed the Richmond Union Passenger Railway, the first successful electric street railway system in the world.

A Toronto streetcar as it would have appeared in 1921. An early form of mass transit, streetcars, which are often called trams or trolleys, still operate in many cities.

DID YOU KNOW?

One of the newest metro stations in Moscow, and the deepest underground, Park Pobedy—or "Victory Park"—has one of the longest escalators ever constructed. With 740 steps, it takes three minutes to reach the top.

Two modern streetcars, from Dublin, Ireland (above), and San Diego, California (below)

THE MALBONE STREET SUBWAY DISASTER

NEW YORK CITY'S SUBWAY SYSTEM was a mere 14 years old and running trains made primarily of wood at the time of one of the worst disasters in mass-transit history. In early winter 1918, Brooklyn Rapid Transit Company management, desperate to find operators due to a strike by motormen earlier that day, ordered subway dispatcher Edward Luciano to drive a train from Brooklyn's Brighton Beach to Manhattan. Luciano had had only two hours of training as a motorman and little sleep that day.

Unfamiliar with the equipment and the route, Luciano took the hairpin turns leading to Malbone Station in Brooklyn too fast (hitting speeds of 30 to 40 miles per hour (48 to 64 km/h) when he should have been traveling no more than 6 miles per hour (9.6 km/h) and hit the brakes too suddenly. The train jumped the track and plunged into a concrete partition between the north- and southbound tracks, crushing the four center cars, while leaving the front and rear cars virtually intact. Two hundred passengers suffered injuries, and 97 lost their lives, many of them decapitated, impaled by shards of wood and glass, or electrocuted by the electricity running through the third rail.

Only in his mid-20s, Luciano went to court, accused of manslaughter. Fortunately for him, the judge acquitted him (ruled him not guilty).

On September 11, 1905, a train on Manhattan's Ninth Avenue elevated line jumped the rails at 53rd Street, killing 12 people and injuring 42. As this wreck shows, not all commuter crashes occurred in tunnels, as did the Malbone Street Disaster.

31

Above, the subway arrives at the Oji-Kamiya Station in Tokyo. Left, one of Tokyo's subway trains. Tokyo's subway system sees nearly 8 million riders on its subway and connected rail lines every day.

In the Underground

In 1863, the world's first subway opened in London. The city of Boston would have a subway route by 1897. It would not be until 1904 that the most famous of them all, the New York City subway, would officially launch. Though the prefix "sub" indicates transportation existing entirely underground, New York has always had both underground and elevated ("el") rails. With close to 660 miles (1,062 km) of track servicing passengers, the cost to build such a subway from scratch today would cost billions of dollars.

Still, cities around the globe have been building their own subways as part of mass-transportation systems, or rapid transit. In recent years, most new systems have been built in Asia, where large population shifts have brought millions of new people into cities. Similar "urbanization" shifts occurred in the United States and Europe early in

More than 5 million travelers speed through New York's subway tunnels each workday. The system, one of the world's oldest, needs constant repair. Some tunnels have been abandoned.

DID YOU KNOW?

Just after Christmas 2006, a group of six men, friends since high school, rode through all 468 New York City subway stations in record time. The *Guinness Book of World Records* recognized the achievement: the Subway Six, as they became known, successfully covered the entire system in 24 hours, 54 minutes, and 3 seconds.

the twentieth century, when subways really caught on. It's no coincidence—many more people can travel efficiently on rapid transit systems than by car or on foot. So, as cities get bigger and more crowded, subways become increasingly important.

LOST AND FOUND

TRAVELERS RARELY BOARD a train empty-handed, but they may exit with fewer items than what they carried onboard. For those looking to retrieve possessions left on trains, many rapid transit systems have a lost and found department. Manhattan's Grand Central Station lost and found keeps items worth less than $100 for 90 days before it gives them to charities or trashes them. Some personal treasures returned to Grand Central include a basset hound and a set of false teeth. The New York City subway system now accepts online inquiries about lost items. In 2008, relieved owners reclaimed more than 40 percent of the 19,000 items listed in the lost and found's computers.

The warehouse-sized central lost and found in Tokyo, Japan, maintained by the police, contains many items forgotten on trains, buses, and taxis. Usually these are umbrellas and cell phones, but wallets and loose money also find their way to the lost and found. In 2002, this made up to a staggering fortune in lost yen. Wallets, envelopes packed with bills, and loose cash added up to approximately 23 million dollars, waiting for their owners to return.

A major restoration project from 1994–1998 returned New York's Grand Central Station to its early glory, and 500,000 daily visitors ensure that it remains a vital city landmark.

A map of the London Underground, the world's oldest subway system, from 1908

Good Night, Sleep Tight

The U.S. Patent Office first registered the invention of a train car with bunk beds in 1838. By the 1850s, Cornelius Vanderbilt's railways included sleeper cars designed by a stationmaster, Webster Wagner. But it was one of Wagner's rivals in the bunk business, George Pullman, who would make his name synonymous with catching "Z's" on a train. A wealthy man and frequent business traveler, Pullman approached the Chicago, Alton & St. Louis line in 1859, proposing new coaches. Pullman sunk $2,000 into the project, which featured upholstered seats that easily converted into beds. This was the birth of the Pullman car. The first car ready for service was named, appropriately, the *Pioneer*.

In 1867, Pullman launched his Hotel Cars. Passengers chose standard sleeping berths, with shared bathroom facilities, or more private sleeping compartments. Uniformed Pullman Porters welcomed passengers, introducing them to the train's services, and helped them pull down the train's upper bunks, the signature stowaway beds. Night owls could relax in the chandelier-lined parlor car, chatting, smoking cigars or playing cards until the wee hours. A Pullman luxury car was part of Abraham Lincoln's funeral train, and his son, Robert Todd Lincoln, became the Pullman Company's second president.

Known for his lavish train cars, sometimes called Palace cars, George Pullman was not universally loved. His harsh actions during the Pullman Strike earned him lasting animosity from train laborers.

A Pullman sleeper car, with typically extravagant furnishings

A first-class Pullman car offered the ultimate in luxury, with richly detailed wood paneling, comfy upholstered chairs, drapery, and even card tables where passengers could pass the time with a game.

THE PULLMAN LEGACY

AN ENTREPRENEUR and a showman, George Pullman gave his luxury creations romantic names such as *Delmonico* and *Marlborough*. He would introduce his new lines with well-publicized cross-country trips. The city of Pullman, Illinois, is named after him. After his death in 1897, the Pullman Company continued to innovate—the *City of Salina*, for example, debuting in 1934, featured air-conditioned cars. The company stopped producing train cars in the 1980s, but Pullman's name still stands out in train history.

SLEEPING AT THE STATION

ALONG THE 72-MILE (116 km) route of England's Settle-Carlisle Railway is Dent Station, which was converted into a small, elegant hotel several years ago. One of the guest rooms of this unique hotel used to be Dent's ticket office. Approximately five trains stop at the station daily. You can watch passengers arrive and depart from your bed.

The world's most famous rail station hotel is the Contemporary Resort in Disney World. Animation pioneer Walt Disney conceived the hotel himself, and it opened in 1971. The showpiece is the Contemporary Tower, a 393-room A-frame building. Disney World's monorail glides through the structure, on its way to and from the theme park.

Located in the picturesque county of Cumbria, Dent Station has been a favorite destination along one of England's most attractive rail lines since it opened in 1877. It is England's highest mainline railroad station, at 1,150 feet (350.5 m) above sea level.

Seeing the World

Traveling by train is sometimes a convenience, sometimes a necessity, and sometimes just plain fun. There's no doubt that many riders enjoy sitting back and enjoying the view, without having to worry about traffic or needing to stop and rest. It didn't take long after railroads started crisscrossing the world for businesspeople to recognize the possibility for profit in this enjoyment. Tourism by train may not be the most popular vacation, but railroads have been carrying curious travelers to beautiful and interesting locations since the end of the nineteenth century.

The Orient Express

Belgian businessman Georges Nagelmackers used his family's wealth and royal connections to create the *Orient Express* long-distance passenger train. The *Orient Express* was as beautiful as the capital cities it connected, with mahogany-paneled compartments and leather seats.

Nagelmackers launched the *Orient Express* in Paris, France, in October 1883. In the ensuing months, he extended the line to Constantinople (now Istanbul, Turkey). Passengers had to board a ferry for the last leg of the journey, but by 1914, the *Orient*

Albert Finney (center) as Agatha Christie's most famous character, Hercule Poirot, questions the snowbound passengers in the 1974 film, *Murder on the Orient Express.*

An *Orient Express* car

MURDER ON THE ORIENT EXPRESS

A FIERCE STORM kept *Orient Express* passengers snowbound near the Balkan Mountains for five days in winter 1929, an incident that inspired the plot of mystery novelist Agatha Christie's *Murder on the Orient Express.* After a man has been found stabbed in his sleeper compartment, Belgian detective Hercule Poirot grills a captive group of suspects, with the train stuck in a snowdrift. In the near-disaster of 1929, there were no casualties, and the passengers eventually reached Istanbul. Christie herself was undeterred by any fear of snowstorms. A year later, she would board the *Orient Express* with her second husband, archaeologist Sir Max Mallowan, for their honeymoon.

Express was making the journey four times a week. World War I, however, halted the train and even after the war ended in 1918, the changing political climate in the countries along its route made rail travel difficult. The *Orient Express* was rerouted several times. By the mid-twentieth century, many potential passengers found air travel more convenient. The *Orient Express*, however, still runs, but on a much shorter route, from Strasbourg, Germany, to Vienna, Austria.

The Orient Express

▦▦▦▦	original route
▦▦▦▦	land route
- - - -	ferry crossing
●	major stops

The Istanbul Sirkeci railway station in Istanbul, Turkey, welcomed *Orient Express* passengers to their final destination from its opening in 1890 to the last train in 1977.

NORWAY

North Sea

SWEDEN

ESTONIA

RUSSIA

LATVIA

LITHUANIA

Baltic Sea

IRELAND

UNITED KINGDOM

DENMARK

BELARUS

London ●

NETHERLANDS   E U R O P E

BELGIUM

GERMANY

POLAND

ATLANTIC OCEAN

Paris

Strasbourg

CZECH REPUBLIC

Munich   Vienna

SLOVAKIA

UKRAINE

FRANCE

SWITZERLAND

Budapest

AUSTRIA

HUNGARY

ROMANIA

SLOVENIA

Bucuresti

Black Sea

BOSNIA

Varna

ITALY

SERBIA

SPAIN

Rome ●

BULGARIA

Istanbul

GREECE

TURKEY

Mediterranean Sea

Ionian Sea

ALGERIA

TUNISIA

DID YOU KNOW?

In June 1842, Queen Victoria became the first British monarch to ride a train, traveling 25 minutes from Slough to Paddington Station, London. She enjoyed the trip so much that she began regularly traveling by train to her expansive country estates.

Queen Victoria

Trans-Siberian Railway

Siberia, a vast, remote region in northeastern Russia, was once known for its isolation. But tourists now find there are things to see between Moscow, Russia, and the port city of Vladivostok, on the Trans-Siberian Railway's impressive passenger routes. The Trans-Siberian's 5,800 miles (9,334 km) of track spans eight time zones and lures adventurers to Siberian attractions such as Lake Baikal, the world's deepest freshwater lake. Close to Vladivostok, on the Sea of Japan, passengers can connect to Asian cities such as Beijing, China, and Pyongyang, North Korea. Workers completed the railway in 1916, after a 15-year effort. Today, the railway's traffic includes freight and passenger trains, as well as privately owned luxury trains in the spirit of the *Orient Express.*

A train speeds along the Trans-Siberian Railroad, offering passengers views of one of the world's great wildernesses.

Trans-Siberian Railway

━━━━━ train route

● terminal city

ARCTIC OCEAN

Moscow

RUSSIA

Sea of Okhotsk

Lake Baikal

Caspian Sea

KAZAKHSTAN

Vladivostok

UZBEKISTAN

MONGOLIA

NORTH KOREA

TURKMENISTAN

KYRGYZSTAN

SOUTH KOREA

IRAN

TAJIKISTAN

CHINA

Yellow Sea

Darjeeling-Himalayan Railway

In 1881, SERVICE BEGAN on the lovely Darjeeling-Himalayan Railway (DHR), connecting Siliguri to the Himalayan city of Darjeeling in India. Before the railroad, Darjeeling suffered major economic troubles. At more than 6,000 feet (1,828 m) above sea level, it was difficult to get essential goods into the city. Merchants for their much sought-after teas needed a better means of distribution. The route's most famous locomotive train was nicknamed the "Toy Train," for its relatively tiny dimensions and ornate interiors. Today, the DHR runs both steam and diesel engines, and it is inexpensive—under $10—for tourists to board.

A Darjeeling-Himalyan Railway locomotive

WONDERS OF THE WORLD, BY TRAIN

YOU CAN SEE BY TRAIN some of the best views of two of the natural wonders of the world. The 104-year-old Victoria Falls Bridge accommodates trains, connecting the African nations of Zambia and Zimbabwe. Spanning 420 feet (128 m) above the Zambezi River, the bridge crosses a gorge near the extraordinary waterfall.

In the United States, the Grand Canyon Railway, which began service in 1901, recently began offering a guided sightseeing trip, in addition to its other rail service. The Coconino Canyon train travels in and around the southwestern red rock wonder. Restored in 1989, the Grand Canyon Railway just celebrated its 90th year of service.

The bridge over the Zambezi River carries trains to a close-up view of the magnificent Victoria Falls, which is one of the world's largest waterfalls.

A Grand Canyon Railway train approaching Williams, Arizona, the main station on the canyon route. The Grand Canyon Railway offers vacations and tours on restored vintage trains—the kind of railway cars you might have traveled in to see the canyon before there were automobiles, plane and helicopter tours, and even paved roads!

Trains in War

Locomotives transformed the way humans waged war in the nineteenth and twentieth centuries. As trains replaced horses, oxen, and wagons, getting material and supplies to combatants became easier. Of course, that made trains and train depots battlefronts themselves, because enemies would try to disrupt supply lines (if ammunition couldn't reach the soldiers, they couldn't fight very well).

Armored Trains

It wasn't just supplies that traveled by train from the 1860s to the 1950s, but soldiers, too. Train stations became places of tearful farewells to departing soldiers and joyful reunions with those who returned.

Soldiers also traveled by train to and from battlegrounds. Designers began adding armor and even weapons to trains that traveled through war zones. Armored trains came into heavy use during World War I, especially in Russia, where trains had to cover a lot of ground and were thus vulnerable to enemy attack. Armored cars have by now nearly completely replaced armored trains, but a few of these trains are still in use.

William Gibbs McAdoo

WORLD WAR I RAILROAD CRISIS

IN THE THROES of a continent-wide conflict, European countries depended on food from the United States to survive. Railroad traffic in the United States went up significantly as cargo traveled to East Coast ports. President Woodrow Wilson brought in his own son-in-law, William McAdoo, to run the United States Railroad Administration (USRA). McAdoo's task was to find a way to get the dozens of railway presidents to curb competition for the greater good. A near-catastrophic shortage of freight cars also threatened the rail system. McAdoo succeeded admirably, and his dedicated management of the USRA was widely praised.

A Russian armored train, complete with gun turrets, from 1919

HIGH SCHOOL RAILROAD

As adult workers headed off to battle, the Illinois Central Railroad began recruiting 16- and 17-year-olds to join its workforce during World War II. Four training schools taught young men the skills to work essential railway jobs, such as brakeman or switchman.

THE ANDREWS RAID

THIS FABLED CIVIL WAR EVENT is also called "The Great Locomotive Chase," with good reason. On the morning of April 12, 1862, Union supporter James J. Andrews and a band of accomplices stole a locomotive, *The General*, deep in Confederate land.

That morning, the locomotive's conductor, William A. Fuller, along with his crew and most of the passengers, had disembarked to eat breakfast at the Lacy Hotel in Big Shanty, Georgia. As they ate, Andrews and his gang snuck onto the waiting train. Soon after, sparks flew, steam hissed, and the train was off. When Fuller saw *The General* begin slowly chugging out of the stations, he bolted from the table and, followed by his crew, gave chase.

Up ahead, Andrews's men destroyed tracks and bridges as they passed on a line crucial to the Confederate's supply routes. After giving chase in other trains and on foot, Fuller was eventually able to board a locomotive called *The Texas*. Once aboard the train, Fuller ordered "full steam ahead"—in reverse! *The Texas* was facing the wrong way on the rails to pursue *The General* in the right direction.

At Ringgold, Georgia, after 14 hours and nearly 87 miles (140 km), *The General* ran out of fuel, and Fuller caught up with Andrews. After his capture and arrest, Andrews was convicted as a spy and executed along with several of his cohorts. Although the plan failed, in 1863, Lincoln's secretary of war, Edwin M. Stanton, met with some of the surviving raiders, who earned Medals of Honor for their loyalty to the Union.

The General **is now on display in the Kennesaw Civil War Museum in Georgia.**

A contemporary illustration shows the raiders torching a train car in an attempt to set a covered railway bridge ablaze and prevent Fuller from catching up with them.

Trains in War continued

During World War II, the Nazis transported millions of Jews and others labeled "undesirable" in crowded, closed boxcars to concentration camps to face forced labor or death.

World War II

During World War II, competing U.S. railroads managed to cooperate in the name of victory. The entire world of industry sacrificed for the Allied effort against fascism—a form of government embraced by Nazi Germany, Italy under the dictator Mussolini, and the Empire of Japan during the 1930s and 1940s. Many railroad workers went off to fight, automobile factories began building tanks and jeeps, and even the Lionel Company stopped manufacturing toy trains to produce compasses for soldiers. Railroads were essential for supply and evacuation, so trains and train depots were vital to the war effort.

The Blitz

In London, citizens found another use for their train system. During World War II, thousands sought refuge in subway stations and tunnels as bombs rained down

Londoners use makeshift beds during the Blitz, when the city's Underground train stations served a new, life-saving purpose.

from German air assaults. Beginning in fall 1940, Nazi forces battered the city and its surrounding areas during eight months of air strikes. This relentless attack is referred to as "the Blitz," from the German word *blitzkrieg*, meaning "lightning war." During the Blitz, as many as 120,000 people could be found seeking safety in the London Underground. Some underground tunnels were not very deep, and scores perished in cave-ins. Britons endured the Blitz with great resolve, but the war would rage on until 1945.

KINDERTRANSPORT

A MONTH AFTER Kristallnacht, a brutal Nazi attack on Jewish communities in Germany and Austria in November 1938, nearly 200 Jewish children from Berlin were brought to the safe haven of western Europe. It was the beginning of the Kindertransport, an operation to rescue Jewish children from areas under Nazi threat. The sealed trains headed to ferries, with the last stop to be Great Britain. The UK government had promised shelter until the children could be reunited with their own kin. But only 1 child in 10 saw their parents after the war. Kindertransport halted after nine months, when Great Britain declared war on Germany. This collaboration of Jewish, Quaker, and other Christian humanitarian groups resulted in the rescue of nearly 10,000 children.

A monument to the Kindertransport stands in Vienna's Westbahnhof train station, the starting point for many Jewish children as they escaped to Britain.

JAPANESE-AMERICAN INTERNMENT

AFTER THE JAPANESE ATTACK on Pearl Harbor on December 7, 1941, unfounded fears of Japanese Americans' sympathy with the Empire of Japan spread. Japanese Americans faced grave discrimination by the U.S. government. Beginning in 1942, more than 100,000 Japanese Americans from the West Coast—men, women and children—were put on trains with darkened windows and armed guards and headed to internment camps, where, although they were not under arrest, they could not leave. Most camps were in remote areas of the mountainous West. In 1988, Congress passed the Civil Liberties Act, which granted former internees $20,000 in restitution and an apology for the injustice of their internment.

Above, Japanese American girls from Los Angeles, aboard a train bound for a War Relocation Authority center. Like many others, they were blissfully unaware of the tough years ahead of them.

Below, evacuees of Japanese ancestry board special trains for Manzanar Relocation Center, 250 miles (402 km) away from Los Angeles, where they had been housed in a War Relocation Authority center. Manzanar, in eastern California, held some 10,000 Japanese Americans during World War II.

Relieved and happy, Japanese American families trail paper streamers form from the car windows of the train that will take them away from the Jerome Center, Denson, Arkansas in summer 1944.

Train Wrecks

We board trains with great anticipation, or merely a shrug. We're off on a visit, or we're just trying to get to work on time. Of course, all modes of transportation are vulnerable to the unexpected: equipment malfunction, fierce weather systems, or human error. Trains are no exception. Though no one can dismiss the importance of trains in modern history or that, on the whole, they've been a most impressive and useful invention, it's also true that since they started running in the late eighteenth century thousands of people have died in train accidents.

Early Train Accidents

In the early days of railroading, collisions, derailments (when a train jumps off the rails), and—for steam trains—boiler explosions caused most train accidents. As with any new technology, it took a while to implement safety features and standards, and without such modern advancements as instantaneous communication, trains could easily run into trouble. On the other hand, trains traveled at slower speeds in those days and carried fewer passengers. Both of these factors contributed to fewer incidents on the rails. Even so, the sad fact is that as soon as there were trains, there were train accidents.

DID YOU KNOW?

A disaster on July 17, 1856, became known as the Great Train Wreck of 1856. The deadliest train accident up to that point, two trains crashed together near Fort Washington, Pennsylvania, killing as many as 67 people, many of them children. The number is uncertain because many of the victims' bodies were never found.

A train crashes through the station at Montparnasse, France, in October 1895, after derailing inside. Killing one person and injuring several others, the accident gave the station some unwelcome fame.

ASHTABULA HORROR

ON THE TRACKS of the Lake Shore and Michigan Southern railway, a 150-foot-long (45 m) iron-truss bridge spanned the Ashtabula Gorge in northeast Ohio. Four days after Christmas, in 1876, the locomotive *Socrates* of the Pacific Express made it over the Ashtabula Bridge— but the cars it pulled did not. Falling 60 feet (18 m) into a creek, the impact set the train's stoves ablaze. Eighty-three people died in what became known as the Ashtabula Horror.

A contemporary illustration of the wrecked train

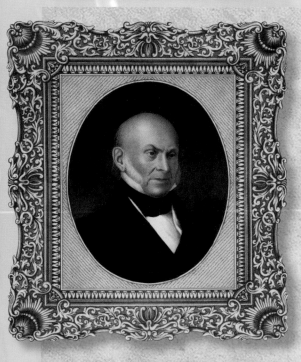

THE CAMDEN & AMBOY ACCIDENT OF 1833

THE CAMDEN & AMBOY wreck is famous not so much for the scope of the disaster as the presence of two public figures who survived it. On a New Jersey-Pennsylvania route, the train carried 66-year-old John Quincy Adams, the sixth president of the United States, and Cornelius Vanderbilt, nearly half Adams's age and already a steamship tycoon. The train's engineer was speeding when the car Adams was riding in lost its grip on the track. The car behind Adams, in which Vanderbilt rode, overturned.

President Adams emerged from the wreck unscathed, but he later wrote about how deeply affected he was by the sight of the desperate victims. Two people died from the impact, and Adams would report that only one person in the overturned car escaped injury. This was not Commodore Vanderbilt, who ended up recovering for months. After the crash, Vanderbilt avoided traveling by train for 30 years—which didn't prevent him from becoming a major railroad tycoon.

John Quincy Adams is the only president to serve in the House of Representatives after leaving the office of the president. It was during his term in the U.S. Congress, as a representative from Massachusetts, that he became a victim of the 1833 train accident.

Tragedy Strikes

By the dawn of the twentieth century, train accidents had become a regular news item. It was the heyday of the Golden Age of Rail, and many more people traveled by rail than ever had before. On the whole, this was great news. Unfortunately, as more people rode the rails, more accidents occurred—not because train safety got worse (in fact, it was getting better all the time), but simply because there were more trains and more opportunities for trouble. Despite everybody's best efforts, accidents are bound to happen sometimes. Occasionally this is due to human error, but often the causes are completely unpredictable. Acts of nature or mechanical failure doom hapless passengers every year.

THE QUEEN OF THE SEA DISASTER

THE DAY AFTER CHRISTMAS 2005, an earthquake in Indonesia triggered a tsunami (a series of large waves brought on by an underwater earthquake or volcanic eruption) that swept through the nation of Sri Lanka. At the city of Peraliya, a 30-foot (9 m) tsunami wave toppled an overcrowded coastal train called the *Sagarika* (or *Queen of the Sea*) as it waited for a signal. Another wave soon followed, scattering the train's eight passenger cabs. Few of the riders had time to escape as water gushed into the cars. A full accounting of victims was never reached in the chaos following the tragedy, but some 1,700 people perished, including both train passengers and villagers who had run to the train for cover. The *Sagarika* did not resume service until 2008.

THE WELLINGTON DISASTER

RUNNING THROUGH the Cascade Mountains of Washington State, fighting off blizzards, might be a regular part of a winter's day on the Great Northern Railroad. But in March 1910, the *Seattle Express* met a foe it couldn't defeat—an avalanche. In the town of Wellington, Washington, scores of passengers and crew were lost as an avalanche sent two trains hurtling into a valley below. Ninety-six passengers and crewmembers lost their lives according to the official count. It still stands as the deadliest avalanche in U.S. history.

The 1910 avalanche swept the mail train and passenger train in Wellington 150 feet (45 m) down, taking with it much of the railroad depot on the way. Quick rescue work by railroad workers saved 23 passengers.

Train crew, firefighters, and other emergency workers watch as a thick cloud of toxic smoke billows from a train wreck in Painesville, Ohio, in 2007. Area residents were evacuated from their homes after the crash released smoke from several hazardous materials aboard the train. In addition to causing injuries and fatalities, train wrecks can also cause massive amounts of damage to tracks, surrounding infrastructure, and nearby buildings or environments—not to mention to the trains involved.

Heists and Heroes

Most train rides are routine: eating, sleeping, and gazing out the window . . . but every once in while, the extraordinary happens. Then it's time for heroes to take the stage—or, sometimes, for villains to make their entrances.

Casey Jones, shown at left and above, leaning out the cab window, with his fireman and close friend, John Wesley McKinnie on the No. 638 train.

A map of the Illinois Central Rail Road, during Casey's time

Casey Jones

One of train history's most famous legends, John Luther Jones hailed from Cayce (pronounced "Casey"), Kentucky, and was nicknamed "Casey" as a young man. On April 29, 1900, this father of four became a legend. A locomotive engineer on the Illinois Central, Jones took over the southbound No. 1 line driving Engine No. 382, a train running more than an hour behind schedule. Leaving Memphis station toward Canton, Mississippi, Jones charged through his route, determined to make up time. Fireman Sim Webb stoked the engine's fire to maintain the locomotive's speed. But just outside Canton, Jones could not maneuver the train around several stalled freight trains. Jones stayed at his post. He ordered Webb to jump and then slammed the brakes. Jones perished in the crash, but Webb and all of the No. 1's passengers were saved.

A roundhouse worker in Canton wrote "The Ballad of Casey Jones" in his honor.

Jesse James

Train legends aren't always about heroes. Although Jesse James only turned to train robbery at the end of a life of crime, he remains one of the most recognizable train villains of all time. A year before his death in 1882, his gang overtook a Chicago, Rock Island and Pacific train in Winston, Missouri, emptying the train's safe and killing the train's conductor. Soon after, at Glendale, Missouri, his gang nabbed more than $10,000 from a Chicago & Alton train.

Newspapers thrived on portraying James as a folk hero, robbing the rich to give to the poor. In reality, James was brutal and reckless—though reportedly he returned money to a woman who had fainted during the Winston heist.

Legendary even during his lifetime, Jesse James now exemplifies the image of the outlaw in America's Old West.

DID YOU KNOW?

A member of his own gang shot Jesse James. His sudden demise allowed con artists to turn his legend to their own advantage by pretending to be the popular train robber.

The last gun ever used by train-robbing legend Jesse James

KATE SHELLEY SAVES THE DAY

THE DAUGHTER OF A CREW FOREMAN for the Chicago & Northwestern railroad, teenager Kate Shelley's heroics on a stormy night in 1881 have inspired many. A locomotive exploring track conditions fell off the Honey Creek Bridge, close to the Shelley farm in Iowa. Kate ran half a mile (0.8 km) in dangerous conditions to the nearest depot. Thanks to her, an oncoming passenger train was stopped before it reached the downed bridge. Not only that, Shelley brought a team back to the crash site, and they rescued two men from the downed locomotive. Shelley's bravery was celebrated in song, and she enjoyed a Chicago & Northwestern rail pass for life.

Kate Shelley

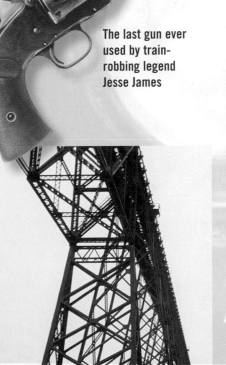

Kate Shelley's name lives on in a railroad bridge named after her, the Kate Shelley High Bridge, near Boone, Iowa. The old metal bridge is currently being replaced by a new concrete bridge, scheduled to open in 2009.

Great Train Robberies

 The railways of England have endured two of the most notorious crimes in history. Both heists came to be known as the Great Train Robbery, though the first, in 1855, is also known as the Great Gold Robbery, and rightly so. Master forger Edward Agar was looking for a major heist. William Pierce toiled in a dismal railway job and aspired to great wealth. Between them they found the South Eastern Railway's gold bullion (bars) train a ripe prize. Together, they devised a painstaking plan to commit the perfect crime.

In the nineteenth century, governments typically used gold to value their currency. Robbers couldn't ask for a more valuable cargo.

SENSATIONAL AND STARTLING "HOLD UP" OF THE "GOLD EXPRESS," BY FAMOUS WESTERN OUTLAWS.

In America's Old West, train robbers typically looked for trains carrying payroll money, but would also force passengers to hand over any valuables.

nabbed him for the crime. Fanny Kay, Agar's common-law wife, turned in Pierce to the police when Pierce failed to give her a share of the loot, as promised by Agar. In total, Agar, Pierce and their accomplices had nabbed the equivalent of $11 million in today's currency.

The Great Gold Robbery

Agar and Pierce brought two more men, a security guard and another rail worker, in on the scheme. Agar copied and replaced the keys that opened the bullion safes. Onboard the train, Agar lifted the gold from the boxes, and then placed lead pellets inside. This would delay discovery of the theft, just in case the boxes were weighed. Unfortunately for the thieves, authorities had their eye on Agar and set a trap that

Sean Connery stars as Edward Pierce in the 1979 film *The First Great Train Robbery*, which was based on the 1855 heist.

Many early train robbers, such as the polite but infamous Bill Miner, known as the "Gentleman Bandit," worked with quantity rather than quality, hitting train after train. After serving prison time in the United States, Miner moved to British Columbia, where he probably committed the Canadian province's first train robbery, in 1904. Miner is said to have been the first robber to use the phrase "Hands Up!"

THE GREAT TRAIN ROBBERY OF 1963

IN AUGUST 1963, in a sleepy English village called Cheddington, a team of robbers overtook a Glasgow-to-London mail train. The train held registered mail and old currency, so old that the British government planned to destroy and replace it. The criminal crew was so skilled, the predawn robbery took only 15 minutes from start to finish, and the bandits made off with about $50 million in today's money. More than a dozen robbers were eventually caught and sentenced to prison.

ATLANTIC OCEAN

SCOTLAND
● Glasgow

NORTHERN IRELAND

WALES

ENGLAND
★ Cheddington
● London

RONNIE BIGGS

A TRAIN ROBBER, a prison escapee, an international fugitive—there has never been a story quite like that of Ronnie Biggs. Biggs eluded authorities for months after the Great Train Robbery of 1963, which took place on his 34th birthday. In 1965, while serving his sentence for his part in the crime, he escaped from an English prison. Biggs was gone, but not forgotten.

Biggs had fled to Brazil, where, in the early 1980s, a group of ex-military men kidnapped him. The kidnappers, hoping to claim a reward for his capture, took him to Barbados. Efforts to have the government of the tiny island nation sign off on his release failed, and Brazilian authorities also refused to send Biggs back to England. Finally, he voluntarily returned to England in 2001. Despite his poor health, Biggs was immediately placed in a prison with the tightest security possible.

A train speeds over the Bridego Bridge near Ledburn, Buckinghamshire. The unremarkable-looking spot was the site of the infamous Great Train Robbery of 1963. Thirteen members of the 15-member gang were caught, including Ronnie Biggs, but most of the money was never recovered.

Trains in Popular Culture

 It could be that you were introduced to rail travel before you ever boarded a train yourself. Thomas the Tank Engine has become a classic television character, and from 1968 to 2001, Mr. Rogers asked children to board the trolley to the Neighborhood of Make-Believe. Trains have also made it from daytime television to the big leagues of Hollywood.

Travel often promises drama, so perhaps it's not surprising that trains have been the setting for many movies. Alfred Hitchcock provided chills in *Strangers on a Train*, Marilyn Monroe snuggled into a sleeper compartment in the 1950s comedy *Some Like It Hot*, James Bond rides the *Orient Express* in *To Russia With Love*, train robbers Butch Cassidy and the Sundance Kid were immortalized on film, and Angelina Jolie fought off bad guys atop a train in *Wanted*. Time and again, our love of trains has been woven into our favorite stories, whether they're told on television, on the silver screen, or in song.

Mr. Rogers and the Neighborhood Trolley

Thomas the Tank Engine, shown here as the star of his own television show, *Thomas and Friends,* has been a popular character in children's fiction since 1946, when he appeared in the book, *Thomas the Tank Engine.*

DID YOU KNOW?

In a classic episode of the hit television show *The Simpsons*, "Marge vs. the Monorail," Marge opposes a planned monorail in Springfield. Talk show host Conan O'Brien wrote the episode.

PRESIDENTS ON TRACK

IN THE EARLY TWENTIETH CENTURY, before U.S. presidents could fly in Air Force One or the helicopter Marine One, commanders in chief relied on rail travel. Franklin Delano Roosevelt traveled more than 200,000 miles (321, 869 km) by train during his four terms in office. The first president to ride the rails was Andrew Jackson, who came aboard the Baltimore & Ohio for a day trip in 1833.

Early twentieth-century politicians didn't just use trains for traveling around. Standing on the back of a train as it stopped in the cities along its route gave candidates a chance to win over voters with speeches, an operation now called a "whistle-stop campaign." Here, President Theodore Roosevelt makes an appearance in Colorado Springs in 1905.

Elvis Presley (1935–1977), also known as "the King of Rock n' Roll," released "Mystery Train" toward the beginning of his career. It is now regarded as one of the King's classics.

TRAINS IN SONG AND DANCE

BEFORE HIS HIT MUSICAL *Phantom of the Opera*, Andrew Lloyd Webber composed *Starlight Express*, a musical comedy about a toy train set. All the actors played trains and performed the entire show on roller skates. Trains must be nearly as much fun to sing about as to ride, because in 1955, Elvis Presley recorded the song "Mystery Train," one of his many, many hits. It would not be the last time a train would take a singer for a winning ride. Perhaps the signature song of Gladys Knight and the Pips was "Midnight Train to Georgia." "Drops of Jupiter" was a hit for a band simply known as Train. Dan Zanes has recorded "Rock Island Line" and "Catch that Train," both preschool favorites. And many other artists, including the Stray Cats and Neil Young have put Presley's "Mystery Train" on their play lists.

The stage play Starlight Express

American Classic

It's not just kids who like trains. Perhaps because trains had such a huge role in U.S. history in the nineteenth and early twentieth centuries—creating tycoons, connecting the country coast to coast, and shaping the face of the nation's cities—rail travel became a major part of American culture. Musicians have immortalized some trains, such as the Atchison, Topeka & Santa Fe, in songs, while the government has paid tribute to trains with stamps for 150 years. Train enthusiasts are everywhere, and you never know when a morning commute will include some famous faces. For example, Vice President Joseph R. Biden acquired the nickname "Amtrak Joe" as a U.S. senator for traveling on the Amtrak train daily from his home state of Delaware to the nation's capitol.

The *Georgia 300*, the train car that carried President-elect Barack Obama and Vice President-elect Joe Biden to Washington, D.C., for the 2009 inauguration.

HONORING TRAINS

FROM THE EARLIEST DAYS of the postal service in the United States, stamps have celebrated personal and technological achievement. On the same day in 1869, the United States Post Office Department (now called the United States Postal Service, or USPS) issued stamps honoring patriot Benjamin Franklin and locomotive travel. In 1952, the Baltimore & Ohio Railroad celebrated their 125th anniversary, dating back to their horse-drawn days, by issuing a commemorative stamp. A three-cent stamp issued in 1944 marked the 75th anniversary of the First Transcontinental Railroad. And in 1999, the USPS honored famous trains of the modern era, including the *Super Chief* and the *Twentieth Century Limited* of the New York Central.

A commemorative United States stamp, featuring a steam-powered train, from 1901

The Barnum & Bailey Greatest Show on Earth

GENERAL VIEW OF THE TWELVE COLOSSAL WATER PROOF CANVAS PAVILIONS, EXACTLY THE SAME AS WILL BE ERECTED, BENEATH WHICH TWO GRAND EXHIBITIONS ARE GIVEN EVERY WEEK DAY. THEY ARE THE LARGEST AND FINEST CANVAS PAVILIONS EVER ERECTED ANYWHERE ON EARTH.

PRINTED IN AMERICA

THE WORLD'S LARGEST, GRANDEST, BEST AMUSEMENT INSTITUTION.

THE CIRCUS TRAIN

BY THE END of World War I, the Ringling Brothers' Barnum & Bailey Circus traveled from city to city in a train 100 cars strong. The Circus Train provided enough room for the company's enormous Big Top tents, more than 1,000 employees, and a veritable zoo of performing animals. In 1956, when the circus decided to perform in large arenas and leave the tents behind, the circus reduced the number of cars to 25.

An advertisement for the Barnum & Bailey Circus, highlighting the massive circus tents and the long circus train needed to carry them

ATCHISON, TOPEKA & SANTA FE RAILWAY

ORIGINALLY STRETCHING ONLY 18 MILES (28 km) from Topeka, Kansas, its trains carrying passengers and coal, the southwestern Atchison, Topeka & Santa Fe Railway was destined for grander things. Railroad founder Cyrus Holliday had set his sights on Santa Fe, years before New Mexico was even granted statehood. The railroad ultimately grew to a 12,000-mile (19,312 km) network, reaching booming cities of the Midwest and West, whistling through places as remote as the Mojave Desert. In World War II, the 713th Railway Operating Battalion, composed of crews of former Santa Fe Railway employees, worked on building and repairing track on fronts in both Europe and Africa. They were better known as the "Santa Fe Battalion." Movie star Judy Garland introduced the song "On the Atchison, Topeka and the Santa Fe," in the 1946 film *The Harvey Girls*. The song became an instant classic.

From 1859-1996, the Atchison, Topeka, & Santa Fe Railway carried its customers through the stark, dramatic landscape of the American Southwest.

Toy Trains

In 1900, trains got smaller. In fact, the cars became as small as a child's hand. That's when inventor Joshua Lionel Cowen launched Lionel, his toy train company. Cowen aimed to make his toy trains look as authentic as possible. For example, his famed Pennsylvania S-2 toy locomotive actually puffs "smoke." When the Great Depression of the 1930s threatened Lionel's revenues, Cowen teamed up with the Disney Corporation's eternal optimist, Mickey Mouse. The wind-up Mickey Mouse Handcar, though it sold for only $1, kept the company going. During World War II, Lionel suspended toy production to make military necessities. Bought by Lionel, LLC in 1986, Lionel has sold more than 50 million trains to date.

Lionel wasn't the only company to make toy trains. In the early twentieth century, with the advent of toy trains (and toy roundhouses, bridges, and switchers), every boy and girl could play a Vanderbilt or Gould and own his or her own fleet. Some people never grow out of their love for toy trains. There are train collector's conventions, and *Model Railroader* magazine is in its eighth decade of publication.

DID YOU KNOW?

The Lionel train company has thrived over the last 10 years under the part ownership of rock superstar Neil Young. Known for such hits as "Heart of Gold"—and for being one-fourth of the musical group Crosby, Stills, Nash and Young—Young developed a keen interest in toy trains while growing up in Canada.

Many people—adults as well as children—enjoy setting up model railroads, or just rolling toy trains along the tiny tracks.

A Lionel locomotive
and coal car

DID YOU KNOW?

One of the most unusual tourist
attractions in Hamburg, Germany, Miniatur
Wunderland is a haven for model trains, cars, and
all things miniature. With as many as 1,300 trains
and approximately 65,620 feet (20,000 m) of track, the
Wunderland displays an impressive collection. In 2005,
the Wunderland constructed the longest miniature
train, with three locomotives and 887 carriages.
A real train with that many cars would be
nearly 6 miles (9.6 km) long!

At right, a richly detailed miniature
train yard, on display at Miniatur
Wunderland in Hamburg, Germany

MONOPOLY MAKES A MILLIONAIRE

LIKE THE RAILWAY TITANS of the nineteenth century, Charles Darrow was in
the right place at the right time. Darrow convinced the Parker Brothers to
mass-produce the game Monopoly in 1933. It turned out that Darrow's game
was something he'd updated but not solely invented. In 1904, Elizabeth
Magie had created the Landlord's Game, in which squares on the board
represented plots of land to purchase. Parker Brothers published two
other games of Magie's in 1937, but it was Darrow who went from being
unemployed during the Great Depression to becoming a millionaire.

Monopoly offers players the chance to own up to four
railroads: the B&O Railroad, the Reading Railroad,
the Short Line, and the Pennsylvania Railroad.

High-Speed Rail

here's high speed and then there's *high speed*. The U.S. government considers any train capable of traveling 90 miles per hour (145 km/h) "high speed." But in Shanghai, China, a passenger train running to and from the city's airport reaches speeds upward of 260 miles per hour (428 km/h). This speedy train travels 20 miles (32 km/h) in less than 8 minutes. Compare that to race car driver Helio Castroneves, who won the 2009 Indianapolis 500's top qualifying spot going no faster than approximately 225 miles per hour (262 km/h). The ambition of high-speed train manufacturers in Europe and Asia is to offer a competitive alternative to air travel wherever possible. And at these speeds, you could say the sky's the limit!

FAST IN FRANCE

BASED IN FRANCE, the abbreviation "TGV" stands for *Train à Grande Vitesse*, or "high-speed train." The first TGV premiered in 1980, and the TGV line is still the world's fastest fleet of passenger trains. High-tech electric motors, large wheels, and tracks with few curves account for the TGV's ability to race. Routes also have very few stations, meaning that the train can roar through areas without slowing down or stopping. The TGV covers France, Luxembourg, Switzerland, Germany, and Belgium and can reach speeds of 200 miles an hour (322 km/h). The popular trains are equipped with modern amenities, including Internet connections and restaurants.

TGV isn't the only high-speed rail in France. In operation since 1994, the Eurostar connects France to England, rumbling under the English Channel through the Channel Tunnel (known as the Chunnel) at speeds of up to 100 miles per hour (161 km/h). By the time the French and British sides of the Chunnel met in 1990, the idea of such a connection was nearly 200 years old. In 1802, French emperor Napoleon I considered a tunnel for traffic between the two countries, but hostilities with England prevented the project.

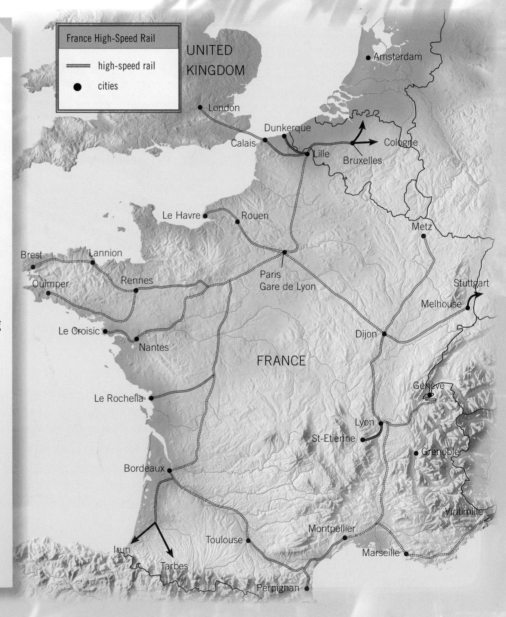

France High-Speed Rail

〜〜〜 high-speed rail

● cities

An Acela waits for passengers to board.

THE EXCELLENT ACELA

ACCELERATION AND EXCELLENCE—put them together and you have the Acela, America's train for the new millennium. The government-owned company Amtrak began Acela service on December 11, 2000, with a route that reaches as far north as Boston and as far south as Washington, D.C. The average speed for the Acela, the fastest train in the United States, is about 84 miles per hour (135 km/h), but on a northern section of track, it can reach a top speed of 150 miles per hour (241 km/h).

DID YOU KNOW?

Meaning "New Main Line," *Shinkansen* is the name for Japan's "Bullet Train" service. Starting in 1964 with the 320-mile (515 km) connection between Tokyo and Osaka, the Shinkansen now covers 1,500 miles (2,414 km) of track. On straight tracks, the train can reach a speed of about 180 miles an hour (290 km/h).

A Shinkansen train

Défense de traverser les voies
Überschreiten der Gleise verboten
Vietato traversare i binari
Do not cross the railway lines

A TGV train pulls into a station.

The Old New High Speed

Long before people started talking about high-speed rail, trains were leading the way for faster and safer transportation. After all, trains were much faster than horses for overland travel and could get from one end of the North American continent much faster than ships, which had to travel either all the way around South America or, after 1914, through the Panama Canal in Central America. Before the transcontinental railroad, a trip from the East Coast to the West Coast could take the better part of a year.

In the twentieth century, airplanes became the new means of high-speed travel. It is only in the last few decades that trains have started to compete with air travel, and they still have a ways to go. But before the first plane took off in 1903 (and it would be many more years before passenger planes became common), trains had ruled as the world's fastest transportation.

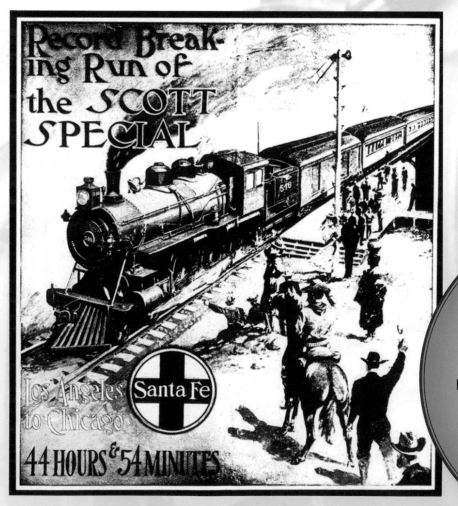

JARRETT & PALMER SPECIAL

CIVIL WAR–ERA theatrical producers Henry Jarrett and Harry Palmer used the railroads to drum up business. One stunt involved their company of actors speeding by rail after a matinee in New York City to perform that night in Philadelphia. Jarrett and Palmer made headlines again in 1876 with a train called the *Transcontinental,* or *Jarrett & Palmer Special.* At a time when a trip from New York to Chicago would often take three days, the *Transcontinental* traveled from Jersey City, New Jersey, to San Francisco, California, in a record-setting four days' time.

"DEATH VALLEY SCOTTY"

In 1905, Walter E. "Scotty" Scott was already famous as a performer in Buffalo Bill Cody's Wild West Show and infamous as a con man. But it was no masquerade when he chartered a Santa Fe locomotive to set a train speed record. On July 9, 1905, the *Death Valley Coyote* (or *Scott Special*) left Los Angeles and arrived in Chicago just under 45 hours later, beating the previous record by more then 7 hours.

FAST TRACK TO BANKING

BY THE MID-NINETEENTH CENTURY, Henry Wells was already a force in express delivery in the East, and aimed to take over the country's entire postal service. It could take the U.S. Postal Service nearly two months to deliver a letter cross-country. Wells teamed with William Fargo in 1852, opening an express delivery and banking business in San Francisco called Wells Fargo. Their typical customers were men who had left families in the East to seek their fortunes in the gold-rich hills of California. Wells Fargo's mission was to safely and rapidly deliver money and letters home and to improve commerce between cities and mining sites. Wells Fargo sent its deliveries by the fastest means possible: stagecoach, steamship, railroad, pony rider, or telegraph. The opening of the transcontinental railroad in 1869 offered Wells Fargo the opportunity to become a truly nationwide express company. At its height, the Wells Fargo express service relied on the rails to connect more than 2,500 cities and towns in 25 states. But private delivery service ended in 1918 during World War I, when the federal government took over all express delivery service. As a result, Wells Fargo turned to banking exclusively, and the company still remains a giant of the industry today.

The Wells Fargo Express Company manned their delivery vehicles with armed guards to protect valuable shipments. Above, the Deadwood Treasure Wagon, loaded with $250,000 worth of gold bullion, leaves the Great Homestake Mine, Deadwood, South Dakota, in 1890.

In the nineteenth and early twentieth centuries, anything that could move faster than a horse was considered "high speed." Today, airplanes and automobiles have regular trains beat hands-down. Still, many travelers prefer to move more slowly while enjoying the view from a train window.

Experimental Trains

 In the 200 years since trains started rolling down their tracks, hundreds of different trains and train types have made their way on the scene. Sometimes a particular problem—such as how to get a train through deep snow—required designers to come up with a new kind of train. Sometimes, improvements mean new or experimental equipment to do the same job better. And of course, trains keep getting faster. The need to make trains run better, more safely, and quicker has encouraged experimentation since the first steam train puffed out its first smoke.

The Fastest Experiment

One of the newest experiments on the tracks is the Maglev train. *Maglev* is short for "magnetic levitation." Electricity powers the trains, and a special type of magnet levitates them. The magnet creates a magnetic field so strong that it can hold a train aloft. (To experience a much weaker magnetic field, try holding two oppositely charged magnets together.) The train is literally floating above the rails, so friction can't slow it down. The Shanghai airport train is the only passenger train in the world using Maglev technology, but the success of experiments with Maglev trains means it might not be alone for long.

A Maglev speed record has never to date been attempted in the United States. Yet two Americans shared the first patent for Maglev technology, Dr. James Powell and Dr. Gordon Danby, whose breakthrough was in superconducting Maglev transportation. Their findings have been applied to the development of the Tokyo-Osaka Maglev route in Japan, scheduled to open in 2025.

DID YOU KNOW?

Though the Maglev speed record is an astounding 361 miles per hour (581 km/h), set on a special run in 2003, the latest TGV is close behind. In April 2007, the TGV's V150 prototype reached 357 miles per hour (575 km/h) in a test run.

Shanghai's Maglev train can reach a top speed of 311 miles per hour (501 km/h).

SPECIAL-USE TRAIN: BUCKER PLOW

TO CONTEND WITH the driving snows of the Sierras during the construction of the Central Pacific railroad, railway designers developed the Bucker plow. A snowplow pushed by several locomotives, the Bucker propelled through snowdrifts that might reach as high as a three-story building. At its best, the Bucker took off like a massive arrow, spraying snow off to the side of the tracks. But the brutal conditions would often get the best of the Bucker, derailing the plow.

It took gigantic snowplows for the Central Pacific Railroad to clear the snowy passes of the Sierra Nevada Mountains in the late 1860s.

RADIOS AND POTATOES

MANY TRAINS HAVE been called "spud specials" over the years—at least, the ones that carried potatoes, which are also called spuds. In 1944, the first train to experiment with two-way radio on board was a "spud special," carrying potatoes from Bakersfield, California, to Chicago, Illinois.

Longyang Station, below, one terminus of the Shangai Maglev

Japan's still-in-developement JR-Maglev

Trains of the Future

By 2030, there could be a billion cars puffing around Earth. That concerns environmentalists (people who work to protect the planet's natural state), because cars release chemicals that trap the sun's heat in Earth's atmosphere, damaging the global climate. Many see speedy trains as a necessary alternative. The other major means of fast travel—airplanes—also pose threats to the environment, and frustrated travelers increasingly clog crowded airports. Though trains probably won't entirely replace airplanes, a train might eventually become the number one choice

Alstom's TGV train may be old news in France, but the future might see many similar trains as high-speed rail takes off.

for landlocked travel. Train engineers are achieving spectacular speeds with both wheel-based and Maglev technology. With luck, clever engineering, and the help of travelers everywhere, the twenty-first century might just see a brand new Golden Age of Rail.

TGV TO AGV

THE COMPANY RESPONSIBLE for the TGV world record, Alstom, is planning to bring high-speed trains to Italy. A newly formed enterprise, Nuovo Trasporto Viaggiatori, will take advantage of Italy's updated rail lines and partner with Alstom and their latest model, the AGV. The letters stand for *Automotrice à Grande Vitesse* ("high-speed self-propelled carriage"). AGVs have no locomotive; the engines are built into the rail cars. The new line will service such cities as Rome and the Olympic city of Torino. One of NTV's investors is Luca di Montezemolo, president of Ferrari, which manufactures some of the fastest cars in the world.

Below, an AGV test run. When the AGV is up and running, it will carry passengers at speeds up to 220 miles per hour (254 km/h).

The sleek nose of the new AGV high-speed train

SUBWAY SYMPHONY

FOR MUSIC AND ART LOVERS, a train station just might be the destination and a means of escape. The New York City subway system brings a modern sophistication to commuting with permanent art installations—a ceramic portrait of Martin Luther King in midtown Manhattan, a mosaic in Harlem, and much more. The program Music Under New York brings professional musicians underground to entertain passers-by. Just past the turnstiles, you might find an opera in progress, some jazz, or the sound of a didgeridoo (an Australian Aboriginal instrument).

A detailed mosaic brightens the view at the subway entrance at the Union Square subway stop in New York City.

Even if they are underground, subway stations don't have to be gloomy places. Above, subway musicians entertain passengers even as a train speeds past. At right, a whimsical shoe-wearing elephant, along with many other sculptures, lighten up the 14th Street subway station in Manhattan, New York City.

Trains of the Future continued

The Detroit People Mover is a 2.9-mile (4.7 km) automated people mover system. It moves on a single-track, one-way loop through the central business district of downtown Detroit, Michigan.

Monorail

Is there still a future for the monorail? The Magic Kingdom thinks so. When the Walt Disney Company built Tokyo Disneyland in the early 1980s (the first Disneyland outside the United States), a monorail, or a train that runs connected to a single track, encircled the park. Tokyo has enjoyed great success with its monorail. Built for the 1964

Olympic Games, Haneda Airport's monorail is extraordinarily popular with travelers to this day. In the United States, the Las Vegas Monorail has been in operation for 15 years. It runs along a nearly 4-mile (6 km) route on the famous "Vegas Strip."

Monorails are sometimes referred to as "People Movers," though a traditional People Mover is different in appearance than a monorail and typically moves fairly slowly along small, fully automated systems. Examples of People Movers can be found at the international airports of New York City, San Francisco, and Newark, New Jersey, and in downtown Detroit, Michigan.

YES WE CAN

IN APRIL 2009, President Barack Obama announced plans to get America up to speed. Committing billions of dollars for the development of high-speed passenger rail lines, the president expressed an urgent need for a "smart transportation system" for the new century. Some of the areas targeted for faster rail service include east-west routes through New York and Pennsylvania, and a Gulf Coast line sweeping through the South.

A monorail

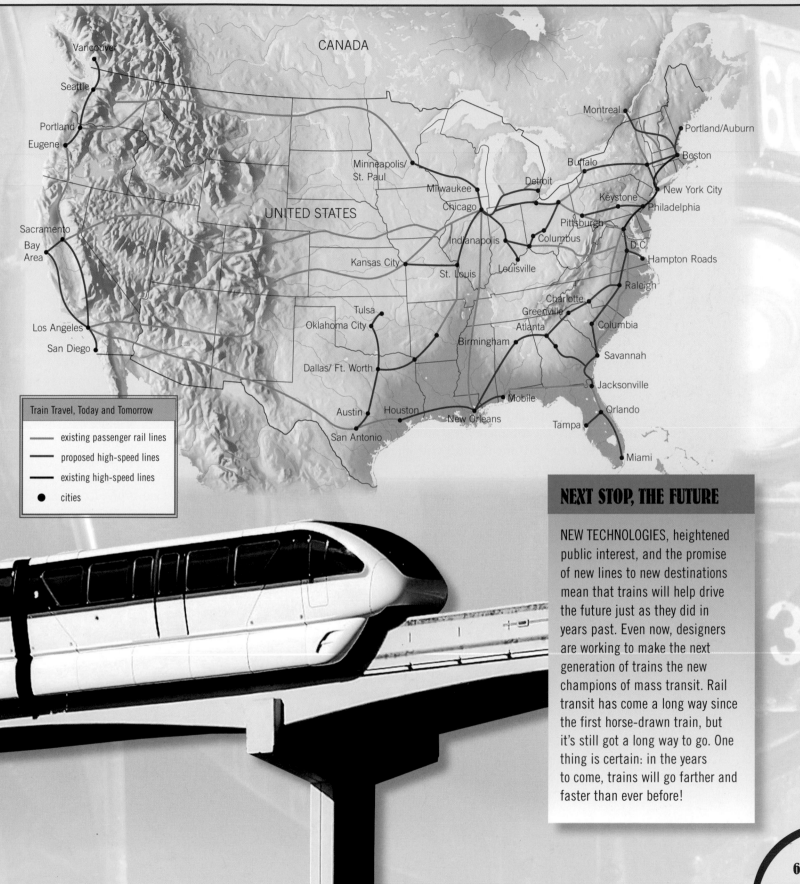

Train Travel, Today and Tomorrow

— existing passenger rail lines
— proposed high-speed lines
— existing high-speed lines
● cities

NEXT STOP, THE FUTURE

NEW TECHNOLOGIES, heightened public interest, and the promise of new lines to new destinations mean that trains will help drive the future just as they did in years past. Even now, designers are working to make the next generation of trains the new champions of mass transit. Rail transit has come a long way since the first horse-drawn train, but it's still got a long way to go. One thing is certain: in the years to come, trains will go farther and faster than ever before!

Find Out More

Words to Know

canal. A man-made waterway for boats. In the early nineteenth century, canals competed with railroads for transportation business.

commuter train. Train intended primarily for people traveling to and from their workplace. Commuter train systems usually focus on a specific city or metro area.

derailment. A type of train accident that describes a train accidentally leaving its tracks

diesel engine. A type of engine that ignites fuel by compressing gas. When the gas is greatly compressed (forced into a smaller and smaller chamber) it heats up and lights the fuel.

First Transcontinental Railroad. Rail line across the United States, completed in 1869. It linked the settled eastern United States with the North American continent's west coast.

freight train. Powerful train designed to carry heavy materials or other goods, including consumer goods and foodstuffs as well as raw industrial materials like coal and iron

Gilded Age. Era of American history roughly corresponding to the 1870s, when the gap between the richest and poorest increased dramatically

Golden Age of Rail. Period of time roughly between the 1870s and 1920s when rail travel peaked in industrialized countries

Golden Spike. Ceremonial spike that officially completed the First Transcontinental Railroad in the United States at Promontory Point, Utah

high-speed rail. Rail system that runs high-speed trains, differently defined by different governments. In Europe, a high-speed train must run at least 124 miles per hour (200 km/h), but in the United States, any train that runs 90 miles an hour (144.8 km) is considered "high-speed."

horsepower. Unit of measurement for power, or how hard an engine can work

Iron Horse. Common term for a train, referring to how trains took over many jobs from horses but were made out of metal

locomotive. Part of a train that provides the power for it to move. Locomotives are sometimes called "engines" because the locomotive carries the train's engine on it.

London Underground. The subway system in London, England, one of the world's most famous subway systems as well as its oldest

Maglev. Technology that lifts trains above their rails by using a special type of extremely powerful magnet

mail train. Train intended to carry mail, a job previously done by horse-drawn transport. Trains still carry mail today, although airplanes and automobiles have taken over most of the world's mail systems.

mass transit. Any system of transportation open to the public. Mass transit systems may include trains, subways, streetcars, buses, and more.

monopoly. Control over an industry or part of an industry. Many railroad tycoons created monopolies over rail lines, transportation, or industries related to railroads, like coal or iron production.